CHI

the true book of

The Moon-Ride Rock Hunt

By Margaret Friskey

CHILDRENS PRESS, CHICAGO

All photographs courtesy of
National Aeronautic and Space Administration
Houston, Texas

Library of Congress Cataloging in Publication Data

Friskey, Margaret, 1901-
    The true book of the moon-ride rock hunt.

    (The "True book"series(Chicago))
    SUMMARY: An easy-to-read description of the
discoveries made on the moon by the Apollo 15 astronauts
who were the first to use a lunar vehicle.
    1. Space flight to the moon—Juvenile literature.
2. Project Apollo—Juvenile literature. [1. Space
flight to the moon. 2. Project Apollo] I. Title.
TL799.M6F75   999' .1   72-1457
ISBN 0-516-01144-8

Library of Congress Catalog Card Number: 72-1457

1 2 3 4 5 6 7 8 9 10 11 12 13 14 15 16 17 18 19 20 21 22 23 24 25 R 75 74 73 72

CONTENTS

This photograph of the earth was taken from 22,300 miles in space. It is easy to see South America a little to the left and below the center of the picture. North America is on the upper left.

THE UNCHANGING MOON

The earth is a ball of rock.

It is spinning through space, taking its moon with it.

The moon is Earth's nearest neighbor in space. But it is more than two hundred thousand miles away.

The moon-god Sin, who was often pictured as a bearded old man with a crescent symbol, was the main Babylonian sky-god.

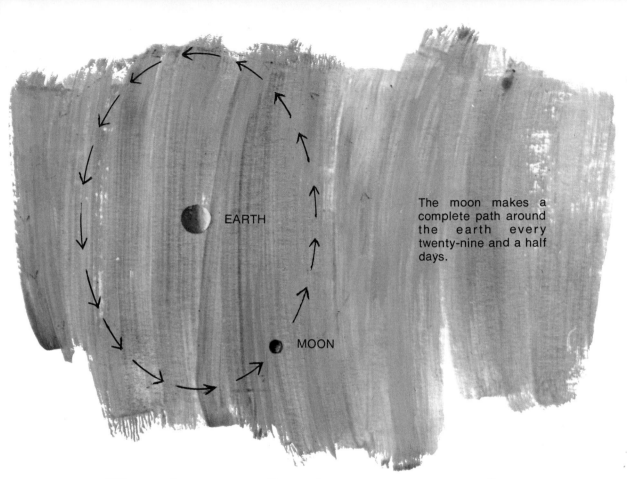

EARTH

MOON

The moon makes a complete path around the earth every twenty-nine and a half days.

For thousands of years no one knew what the moon was made of.

Early people feared it. Some of them worshipped it.

Later, men studied it. They charted its path around the earth.

Then, about four hundred years ago, Galileo built the first telescope.

Telescopes made it possible for men to see the mountains, valleys, and plains on the moon.

They could see things that made them think that the mountains, valleys, and plains on the moon did not change.

Later, unmanned spaceships sent back pictures of the moon.

Men studied the pictures.

They called the plains *seas*.

They called the deep cuts in the rock *rilles*.

They gave names to the mountain ranges.

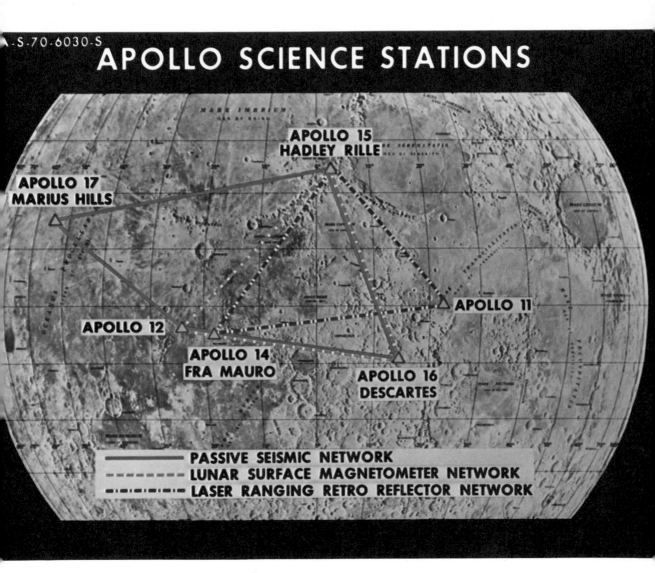

APOLLO SCIENCE STATIONS

A-S-70-6030-S

APOLLO 15
HADLEY RILLE

APOLLO 17
MARIUS HILLS

APOLLO 11

APOLLO 12

APOLLO 14
FRA MAURO

APOLLO 16
DESCARTES

——————— PASSIVE SEISMIC NETWORK
– – – – – – LUNAR SURFACE MAGNETOMETER NETWORK
–·–·–·–·– LASER RANGING RETRO REFLECTOR NETWORK

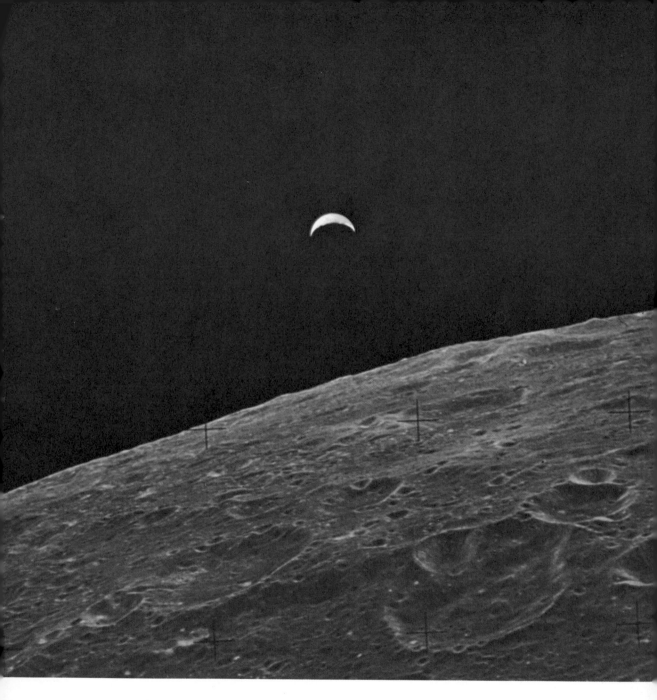

The crescent of Earth shows above the moon's horizon.

They believed, or inferred, from what they could see, that the moon has no air.

So there would be no wind.

They believed that the moon has no water.

So there would be no rain, nor ice, nor rivers.

Men inferred that there were no living things on the moon.

The first men landed on the moon in 1969. They found that what was believed about the moon was true. Each time man has explored on the moon he has learned more about it.

There are still mysteries about how Earth and moon and solar system were formed. There is more to be learned.

The story is being read in rocks. Some of the stories are told in the unchanging rocks and mountains of the moon.

The unchanging rocks and mountains of the moon will help man learn more of the story of how the earth and the moon and the solar system were formed.

The lunar roving vehicle (LRV), commonly called the Lunar Rover, was the first kind of transportation used by men who landed on the moon. Until the Apollo 15 flight in 1971, men on the moon had to walk to wherever they wished to go. In the Rover, they were able to go much greater distances than ever before.

16

THE LUNAR ROVER

David Scott and James Irwin were the fourth pair of astronauts to land on the moon.

They were the first to take along a moon buggy called the *Lunar Rover*. This was on the Apollo 15 flight in 1971.

In the Rover they could ride over the rough surface of the moon. They could go several miles to hunt for rocks.

They believed that the surface of the moon does not change. They hoped to find a rock as old as the moon.

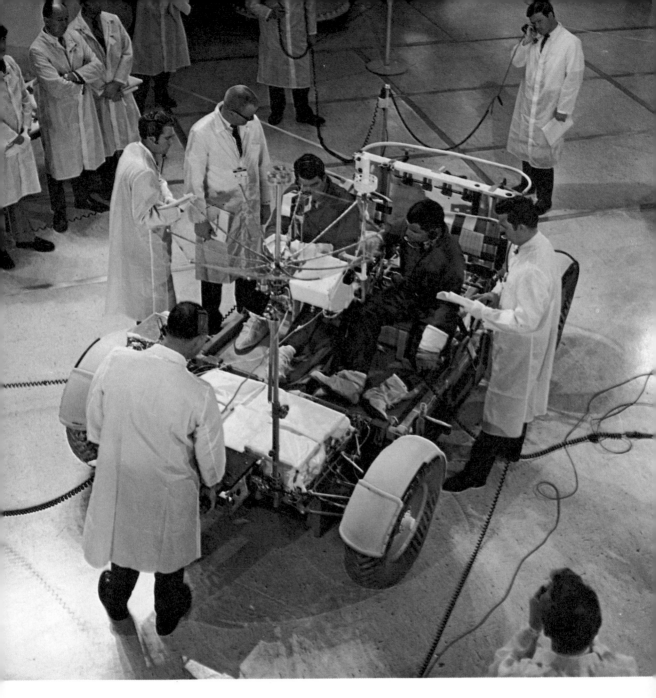

Four Lunar Rovers were built by the Boeing Company. Three of these Rovers were built to be used as flight vehicles to transport astronauts during the Apollo 15, 16, and 17 missions. This Rover was a "qualification unit," tested to prove that the Rover would meet the NASA specifications.

Apollo 15 astronauts James Irwin, David Scott, and Alfred Worden display the battery-powered Lunar Rover. It is equipped with a television camera that will be used when the Rover is parked. The camera can be controlled from the ground while the astronauts are exploring the moon.

Apollo 15 astronaut James B. Irwin explains the Lunar Rover during a press conference.

THE FIRST RIDE

Scott and Irwin climbed into the Rover. They fastened their seat belts.

Scott found that he could not steer with the front wheels. On this first ride he had to steer with the back wheels.

"This is like steering a boat," he said.

Irwin on the moon with the Rover. Nearby is the lunar module *Falcon*, which was the astronauts' "home" on the moon.

The Rover was so light on the moon that the astronauts had a hard time keeping it on the ground. Here, it looks as if both the Rover's rear wheels are entirely off the ground.

They bounced away through six inches of rock dust.

They headed toward the slope of the Apennine Mountains.

"Hang on!" cried Scott.

"Bucking bronco!" said Irwin.

Men and car weighed so little on the moon that the car hopped along. The men were in danger of being tossed out.

Their seat belts kept them in the Rover.

The men could see the Apennine
Mountains. They rose more than two
miles above the surface of the moon.

Astronauts Irwin and Scott could see the Appenine Mountains in the distance.

This view of Hadley Rille was taken through the lunar module window after liftoff.

Scott and Irwin came to a deep gorge.
It looked like a cut in the rock.

"Hey! There's the rille!" said
Irwin.

Hadley Rille was a half-mile wide, six
hundred feet deep, and sixty miles long.

There it was, just as they had seen
it on the photograph taken from space.

The far side was steep. There were
large rocks scattered over it. It looked
as if the rille had been made by flowing
lava.

The men rode on to Elbow Crater.

They got out of the Rover and hopped along in clouds of dust.

The rocks they found had glasslike crystals in them. Such rocks are made by heat.

They could see Mount Hadley in the distance. It rose almost fifteen thousand feet above the plain.

The astronauts had an excellent view of Mount Hadley as they hunted for rocks on the moon.

St. George Crater looks like a big round hole in the slope of the mountain.

The men could see St. George Crater. It looked like a big round hole in the slope of the mountain.

They rode toward it on their rock hunt.

When they reached the crater, they gathered more rocks to bring back to earth.

"Imagine," said Scott. "These rocks were here before creatures lived in the sea or roamed the land."

Scott and Irwin finally started back to the *Falcon*. This was the lunar module that was their home on the moon.

It was all downhill going back.

Scott stopped and got out of the Rover. He tried to drill a ten-foot hole for an experiment. The experiment would measure heat from within the moon.

He worked and worked. But he could drill through only three or four feet.

"I'll tell you one thing," he panted. "This base is firm."

Scott is working very hard trying to drill into the surface of the moon.

Closeup view of some of the large rocks found on the moon by Scott and Irwin.

THE SECOND RIDE

Scott and Irwin set out again the next day in the Rover. They headed for Spur Crater. It is on the slope of the Apennine Mountains.

They spotted a big rock with crystals in it. This was an exciting find. It seemed to be more proof of early volcanic action on the moon.

This is the oldest rock yet found on the moon. It is thought to be more than four billion years old.

It is almost as old as the moon, but not quite. It may help prove that the moon has changed very little since it was formed.

THE THIRD RIDE

Scott and Irwin set out on their last ride on the moon. They rode along the rim of Hadley Rille again.

"Somebody has been here," said Scott. They could see their own tracks from their first trip. There was no wind or rain to rub them out.

As on other rides, wonderful pictures of the unchanging mountains of the moon were sent to Earth by television.

The astronauts' bootprints show up very clearly in this picture. The prints will remain on the moon for a long, long time, as there is no wind or rain there to rub them out.

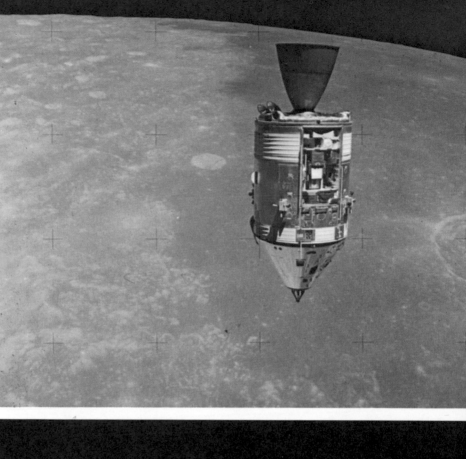

These pictures of the Apollo command and service modules were taken from the lunar module. The picture at the top of the page shows the service module's scientific instrument module (SIM) bay.

Scott and Irwin spent almost three days on the moon.

They traveled about fifteen miles along the Apennine Mountains. They gathered 173 pounds of rocks.

All this time, Alfred Worden orbited the moon in the command module. He had to wait for the *Falcon* to return the men to the mother ship for the trip back to Earth.

He took many pictures of the moon. Pictures of the far side of the moon showed great fields of cinder cones. These seem to show that the moon was once so hot that it was molten.

Craters on the far side of the moon.

Astronaut Irwin salutes beside the American flag on the moon. The lunar module *Falcon* is in the center of the picture, and the Rover on the right.

Scott and Irwin, rock hunters on the moon, had a most successful trip. More was learned about the moon in three days than had been learned in hundreds of years.

Left to right: Apollo 16 astronauts Thomas K. Mattingly II,
command module pilot; John W. Young, commander; and Charles
M. Duke, Jr., lunar module pilot.

The lunar module *Orion* and the Lunar Rover
at the Apollo 16 Descartes landing site.

Astronaut John W. Young gives the Rover a
speed workout on the first trip Apollo 16
astronauts took outside the *Orion*.

APOLLO 16

In April of 1972 the Apollo 16 astronauts landed in the Descartes area of the moon. Commander John W. Young and Lunar Module Pilot Charles M. Duke, Jr. were the second pair of astronauts to take a Lunar Rover along during a flight to the moon.

Astronaut Charles M. Duke Jr. examines closely the surface of a large boulder at North Ray crater during one of the Apollo 16 rock-hunting expeditions.

ABOUT THE AUTHOR

Margaret Friskey, Editor Emeritus of Childrens Press, was Editor-In-Chief of the company from its conception in 1945 until her retirement in 1971. It was under her editorial direction that Childrens Press expanded to become a major juvenile publishing house. Although she now has more free time, her days are by no means quiet. She spends time with her children and grand-children, all of whom live near enough to her little house in Evanston to visit often. She also has more time to concentrate on her writing. With the publication of two new books in 1972, twenty of her books have been published by Childrens Press.

ABOUT THE ARTIST

"I try to make my artwork as 'alive' and easy to identify with as possible," Tom Dunnington explains. He is keenly aware of the importance of sensitivity and communication in art. To heighten his own awareness he has become active in the Human Potential Development Movement, leading encounter groups. He has illustrated many books for Childrens Press, done textbook work, and is a regular contributor to "Highlights for Children."